Michèle Matteau

Portals of Memory

Translated by Paul Savoie

BookLand press

Published by BookLand Press
15 Allstate Parkway, Suite 600, Markham, Ontario L3R 5B4
www.booklandpress.com

Printed in Canada

Library and Archives Canada Cataloguing in Publication

Matteau, Michèle, 1944-
[Passerelles. English]
Portals of memory / Michèle Matteau; translated by Paul Savoie.

Translation of: Passerelles.
Poems.
Issued in print and electronic formats.
ISBN 978-1-77231-026-9 (paperback).--ISBN 978-1-77231-027-6 (epub).--
ISBN 978-1-77231-028-3 (pdf)

I. Savoie, Paul, 1946-, translator II. Title. III. Title: Passerelles. English

PS8576.A8294P3813 2016 C841'.6 C2016-900048-6
C2016-900049-4

Canada Council for the Arts Conseil des arts du Canada

ONTARIO ARTS COUNCIL
CONSEIL DES ARTS DE L'ONTARIO
an Ontario government agency
un organisme du gouvernement de l'Ontario

We acknowledge the financial support of the Government of Canada through the National Translation Program for Book Publishing, an initiative of the *Roadmap for Canada's Official Languages 2013-2018: Education, Immigration, Communities*, for our translation activities. We acknowledge the support of the Canada Council for the Arts, which last year invested $153 million to bring the arts to Canadians throughout the country. We acknowledge the support of the Ontario Arts Council (OAC), an agency of the Government of Ontario.

To those whose voice
can no longer be heard

Table of Contents

Absent Ones

They anchor me to firm ground
to the soiled snow of pitiful streets
to powdery fields
bloated by haughty July

They shackle me
to spongy peat
to the oozing clay of departures

They dress me with ochre and pink sandstone
with granite cliffs
dry wave-worn pebbles
solstice-pearled glaciers

They forbid mourning
and even the vibrant shimmerings of words

They fail to align
the muzzled cones
of cypress shadow of night

They wrap me inside the knot
of hope-stained illusion

Still scorching
the volatile mist
breaks free from comets
entangled in their own hair

Fingers enmeshed in childhood's ribbons
refuge against the initial onslaught of aloneness
shoulder on which to lament the spoils of awakening

Messengers of wind
rooted in sand dunes
attempting to free themselves
from tempest's talons

Atrophied thoughts
still-born poems
stifled sounds
in word's gullet

Scattered specks of light
gutted shells
resonating in the abyss

With each unrelenting
passing of hours
wanes the comfort of certainties

All too brief life patches
arrows of glowing embers
trapped inside the meanderings of memory

Loved ones   cherished ones
roads left behind
without the solace of farewells

Passages

Dawn

Your laughter seeped
through branches
disrupted the silence of the river

At the wilted extremity of night
you sorted through the secrets of time
to taste things to come

On the naked rocks of May
at the dull stone walls
your hands scattered sea mists
to ignite the phosphorescence of chalices

After the blazing fires of autumn
your gardens curled inward
into the round ruddiness of hydrangeas
and the frightened mauve of the aster

Inside the loft of winter
you made use of felt and straw
velvet and satin

Amid fruit and flowers
leaves and feathers
the pastel silk of "follow-me-young-man"
the faceless heads of hatted forms
lingered in the frost
hoping to seduce spring

Then one day
nothing

No gardens for your hands
no river for your gaze
nor ribbons for your hats

Nothing but the chrysanthemums
of deceitful September

And at times night's resounding
where for an instant
glows your emerging laughter

Morning

Do trees preserve traces
of the bark that enfolds them?

Does the stone remember
the caressing hand?

In the wintered mountain
where do snow's traps lie?

Why...

So many comings and goings
and not a single trace of trampled grass!

When pearls are ripped
from the necklace's embrace
do they go on drumming
against the panes of memory?

Do knitted things
fall prey
to time's unspooling?

Ravaged by futile waiting
forced to make do with morsels
in fearful morning's breath
you sought refuge in precarious gasps

You found yourself in the throes of an uncertain fate
without the solace of defiant noon

Silence swallowed your name whole

Midday

Spirals coil
around the bed of ferns
the midday wind
lifts the horse's mane

The bow tunes its gallop
on the cello's taut strings

Clusters forming
on their layered horizons
incandescent coals in triolets
on the verge of ascending

Caught between ivory and ebony
I let the notes swirl me
beyond the musical keys
into an ephemeral pas de deux

You cannot leave
the camp of horrors
the bloody granite quarry
where to become invisible
your youth donned the reaper's vestment

Cruel whip
curare of the incendiary word
canon mouths set off
stateless echo of disgust
where the unthinkable remains ripe
with all that is inhuman

You freely navigate
between foreign shores

Forever dragging along the fiery ball
cutting off all escape routes

Night after night
your hatred
helps you to survive

And you wait
for the white flag to quiver
allowing you to become human once again

Dusk

Between two 'maybes'
served up by folly
your knotted insides churned

You lost faith in your hands' power
to hold on to anything

You avoided mirrors
in order to escape your tarnished image

You whose table eased hunger
whose ears had always remained alert
you now found refuge
in pain's deaf solitude

Trapped inside dull dusk
you were reduced
to a soulful cry

A lament
writhing in the ashes
of a final illusion

Evening

No more vocal exercises
at the break of day

No more movement
from full notes to half notes
on morning's perilous scale
when your voice broke out
between rest and breath
on time's continuum

Between soaked leaves
I still make out
the sound of horns
the cry of the doe at bay

In the absurd gyrations of an aria
opera's golden calf offers resistance
calumny accentuates its crescendos
through prophetic vibratos

I remember...

Roadside songs
gushing melodies
in the hazy quietude of Sundays
Easter rituals resounding
Holy Night harnessing the wintry wind

You cast off imagined villages
where mean-spirited men lurked

You gave them glimpses
of the gaping abyss
behind their shattered glass

They never forgave you

Torn asunder
your dreams were hanged
from disillusion's gallows

Only a drizzle of rainbows
remains
above April's falls

Though your voice intermittently rings out
at the bend of other worlds
the childhood's veneer
gradually fades

Soon I will have the same age as your death

Night

Though your life was filled
with exotic perfumes

You floated way
on the sea's hazy amethyst

You crafted streamers
to ward off tedium

Your flights of fancy were strong enough
to distil dreams

Your wanderings drew
star-speckled fields

You christened
each display of sidereal brilliance
garlanded chimera's dance
with its aura

Imperceptibly
between twin shooting meteors
the day shelled your Shangri La's

Frigid truth lashed out...
you were no longer quite here

Your body was draped
in the imperfect jaundice of departure

Death settled into
the polished surfaces of your hideaway

Deprived of your voice
distant stars
fell silent

On this August night
with shooting daisies raining down
from the Milky Way
I can almost hear
the ancient incantation
Sirius
Vega
Rigel
Antares
Betelgeuse

Over time's translucent void
tirelessly
you set your stars ablaze

The Wait

Its name instils fear
even in the belfry bells

Unfazed
it deepens the wrinkles
on my ever-furled brow

The reaper of empty spaces
moves along the path
hardened by sinister drums

With slow insidious intent
it crawls
usurping my childhood games

It wedges itself
inside the willow's frescoes
sets the undergrowth abuzz
with its irresistible drone

First with rain and then seepage
at dawn's break
it floods the stand of street lamps

It burrows its way into my skin
gorges itself with my blood
clutters the portals of memory

Will I be given enough time
to figure out who I am?

To avoid the inescapable funeral march
though briefly
I insert myself
inside its clammy shadow

What once turned me on
now rubs me out

I am torn apart
by a treacherous faith
slowly being eaten away

Beyond the fantastic tales
where lingers the patience of a thousand and one nights
behind the protruding rock I believed unmovable
at the equinox of March
inside summer's dizzying bolero
on autumn's mosaic
I know my winter abides

The irrelevant greyness
of ruts
engulfs me

The ground beneath me shakes
within the hoarse folds
of its flow

The reverberating tap tapping
of future hurricanes
unhinges me

Drumbeats from a forest storm
mingle with a screeching of sirens
a blood-soaked hunt
the din of an apocalypse
averting the funambulist's distress

Even now
the blueness of its night sky
draws me in

Even now
I am inebriated
by the thrust of vertigo

Its insolent timpani
beat against silence's eardrum

And so
silence
is subdued

The abyss continues to resist
I die in waiting

The comforting mirage
from parallel universes
spreads into
the unknotted horizon

Face to Face

My skin is torn
by the claws of others

I no longer decipher images
that once offered meanings so clear

The gaze's naked sword
splits the charcoal pencil of uncertainty

The utterances of intimacy dry up
all imprints of trysts vanish

The past fades away
tramples the present

When there is no one
to retain the given word
it shrivels up
like bed sheets inside a disappearing room

Locked inside the turbulence
I stumble at the crossroads

I fall back
on stammerings of candour
shouting one last time
I believe

But only in
the inexorable power
of life

Faith woven
in sun and rain
perverse juggling
in the court of miracles

I know
nothing

I am
nothing

I am not
a player
in the act of transforming worlds

Even without me
the river's foil unfolds

Even without me
the leaf dances inside dawn's open palm

Even without me
the sun's ardour reddens the eye of the lake

Even without me
impervious
the shuttle of time threads incessantly
through the framework of its return

On its endless expanse
I dare trace
the gold edges
of a moment's awareness

Thus the vivid dust of its passing
becomes iridescent on the tips of the hourglass

With cutting slowness
it releases its twin helix
and affixes itself to the alabaster tentacles
of a wandering galaxy

So that
all things
can begin anew...

About the Translator

Paul Savoie is one of Canada's most prolific authors, writing in both French and English. Originally from Saint-Boniface, Manitoba, he has lived in Ontario since the early 1970s. He has written more than 30 books, including several collections of poetry, short stories, and translations. His poetry books, *Crac* and *Bleu bémol,* both won the Trillium Book Award. Involved in the arts community for more than 25 years, Savoie also composes music for the piano. He has worked for the Canada Council for the Arts, the Ontario Arts Council, and the Canadian Television Fund. He lives in Toronto, Ontario.